ANCIENT LANDSCAPES OF THE GRAND CANYON REGION

LECTOR HOUSE PUBLIC DOMAIN WORKS

ANCIENT LANDSCAPES OF THE GRAND CANYON REGION

EDWIN DINWIDDIE MCKEE

ISBN: 978-93-89821-89-5

Published: 1931

LECTOR HOUSE LLP
E-MAIL: lectorpublishing@gmail.com

THE GRAND CANYON.

1. SCHISTS AND GRANITES (ARCHEAN ERA): 2. SANDSTONES, LIMESTONES, SHALES (ALGONKIAN ERA): 3. TONTO FORMATIONS (CAMBRIAN PERIOD): 4. REDWALL LIMESTONE (MISSISSIPPIAN PERIOD): 5. SUPAI SANDSTONE AND SHALE (PERMIAN PERIOD): 6. HERMIT SHALE (PERMIAN PERIOD): 7. COCONINO SANDSTONE (PERMIAN PERIOD): 8. TOROWEAP AND KAIBAB FORMATIONS (PERMIAN PERIOD).

NATIONAL PARK SERVICE

ANCIENT LANDSCAPES OF THE GRAND CANYON REGION

THE GEOLOGY OF GRAND CANYON, ZION, BRYCE, PETRIFIED FOREST & PAINTED DESERT

BY

EDWIN D. MCKEE,

Asst. Director
Museum of Northern Arizona

SKETCHES AND CHARTS BY LOUIS SCHELLBACH 3RD PARK NATURALIST, GRAND CANYON NATIONAL PARK, AND RUSSELL HASTINGS

1931

CONTENTS

LIST OF ILLUSTRATIONS

INTRODUCTION

Probably no place in the world of similar area has recorded a more complete or a more interesting resume of the earth's history than has the high plateau country of northern Arizona and southern Utah. Although many great events and some long intervals of time are not represented by the formations of this region, yet of the five major chapters or eras into which all of time has been divided by geologists, at least some parts of each have left their traces in this area.

Whether on the brink of the mighty Grand Canyon, among beautiful logs of the Petrified Forest, or beneath the lofty walls of Zion—the "Rainbow of the Desert"—one looks upon rocks which are not alone curious or colorful, but which are also records of the past inscribed and illustrated in an intensely interesting manner. In one place is seen the sand of ancient dunes, in another the border of an early sea, or perhaps the floodplain of mighty rivers, and in all of these remain the unmistakable evidences of life—plants and animals preserved to make a reality of the living, moving past. Everywhere are found the evidences of those great processes of nature—erosion of the high country, land formation in the low country, and mighty crustal movements slowly raising or lowering the land in both.

From the rim of Grand Canyon one not only looks down through tremendous space, but also through time, glimpsing the record of vast ages, measurable not in centuries but in millions and even hundreds of millions of years. There in the bottom of that mighty chasm are found rocks formed during the first and oldest era—rocks in which the original structure has been entirely modified by great heat and pressure and in which no evidence of life has been found. There in the Grand Canyon are also seen two other great series of rocks, those of the second era which are partially altered and which contain earliest traces of plants, and those of the succeeding era in which are preserved primitive animals of many types.

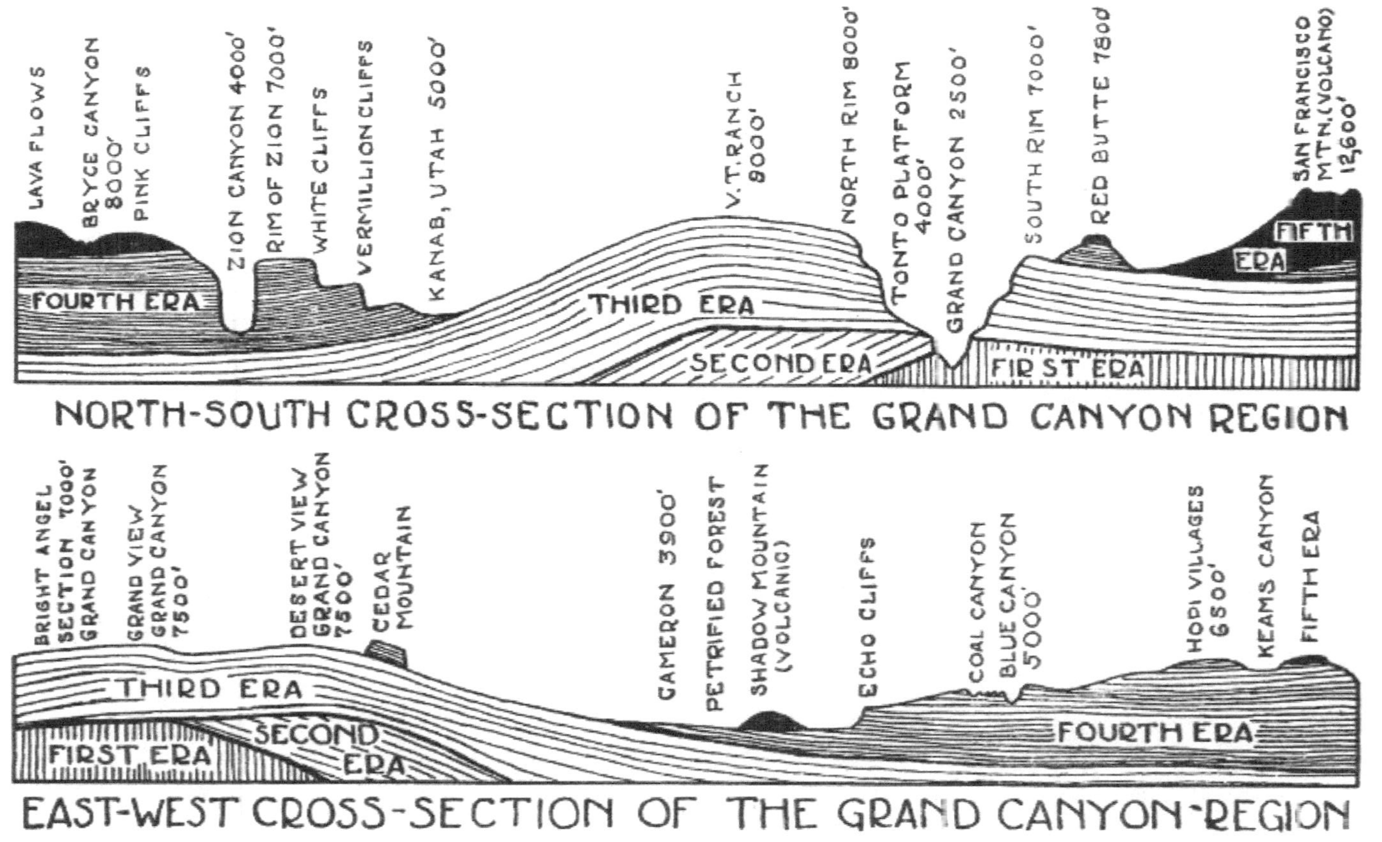

DIAGRAMMATIC SECTIONS OF GRAND CANYON REGION

Rocks of the fourth great era—the age of dinosaurs—lend color to the Painted

Desert, and to the sheer walls of Zion Canyon. Beautiful little Bryce Canyon to the north boasts of some of the most recently formed rocks in the region—those of the fifth and last era, the age of mammals. The great volcanic mountains and the marvelous features of erosion, such as the canyons and the desert cliffs, are also developments of this most recent chapter. In brief, the Grand Canyon region affords some wonderfully interesting glimpses of ancient landscapes during many different parts of the earth's history, and these make the past a moving, living thing.

CHAPTER I
THE ARCHEAN ERA

ROCKS OF FIRST ERA. INNER GORGE OF GRAND CANYON

THE EARTH'S OLDEST ROCKS (THE ARCHEAN ERA)

Looking into the depths of Grand Canyon from any point within the Bright Angel section, one is immediately impressed by the narrow V-shaped gorge cut in the black rocks at the bottom. This is popularly termed the Granite or Inner Gorge. Within its walls one is in another world, both scenically and geologically. Their steep, bare sides, whose surfaces are chaotic in the extreme, have a history—long and complex. The rocks of which they are formed—some of the oldest known today on the surface of the earth—partially tell the story of the first great era in geologic history.

Other rocks of this, the Archean age, are found in the Rockies, in the Adirondacks of New York, and to a very great extent in eastern Canada. In the last named place they contain valuable deposits of iron, nickel, cobalt, and copper. Rocks which probably also correspond in age occur in Scandinavia, Brazil, China, India, and central Africa.

At the Grand Canyon, although we are impressed by the depth of the dark Archean rocks, beneath the plateau surface approximately a mile, yet we marvel even more when we contemplate their great age and the important series of events whose history they partially record. Built up originally as great horizontal deposits of sand and mud, they were bent by mighty crustal movements until high mountains, probably comparable to the present Alps, were formed. Pressures from the northwest and southeast apparently folded them. The rocks themselves were greatly compressed and heated, with the result that complete recrystallization and the development of a banded structure were brought about. The present vertical attitude of these ancient beds, together with their dense crystalline character, is evidence of the great depth at which they were formed and of the extreme pressures to which they were subjected. In brief, the rocks that we see today in the Canyon bottom represent merely the roots of once lofty mountains, and the flat surface cut on these rocks is an old plain that resulted from the wearing down of high country in this region.

BLOCK DIAGRAMS OF EVENTS OF FIRST ERA

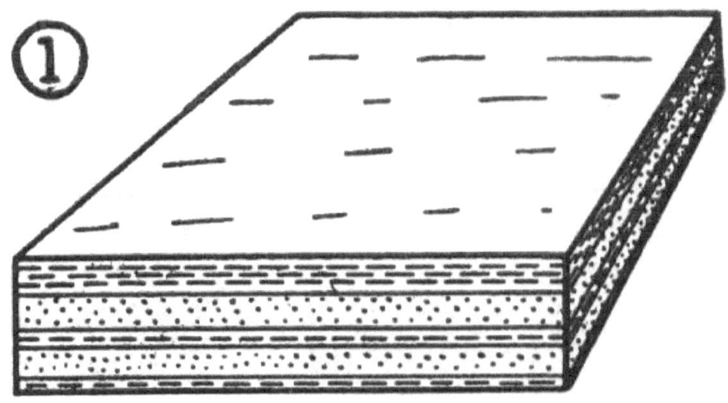

1 SANDS AND MUDS ACCUMULATED TO FORM ROCK STRATA.

2 THE STRATA WERE FOLDED INTO HIGH MOUNTAINS. HEAT AND PRESSURE CHANGED BOTH STRUCTURE AND COMPOSITION OF THE LOWER ROCKS DURING THE FOLDING.

3 MOLTEN MASSES WERE FORCED UP INTO CRACKS FROM BE-LOW. UPON COOLING THEY FORMED LAVAS ON THE SURFACE

AND GRANITES BENEATH.

4 DURING A TREMENDOUSLY LONG PERIOD OF TIME THE RIVERS AND RAINS SLOWLY WIDENED THE VALLEYS AND WORE DOWN THE ANCIENT MOUNTAINS TO A GREAT PLAIN NEAR SEA LEVEL.

As yet no definite traces of either plant or animal life have been found in rocks of the Archean age in Grand Canyon. Though various forms of life may have existed then, and may have been preserved in the original rocks, their record has since been entirely removed by those extreme pressures which altered even the composition and structure of the rocks themselves.

GRANITE IN GRAND CANYON (THE ARCHEAN ERA)

Within the black, crystalline rocks of the Inner Gorge may be seen many large streaks, bands or irregular masses of a lighter color. From the Canyon rim these appear white, but from nearby they are usually pink. These light colored rocks are granites with a coarse crystalline texture.

Granites derive their name from their granular texture. They are formed by the slow cooling of molten masses that have been forced into older rocks from the earth's interior. From a similar source are formed lavas and volcanic ash, but these flow out or are ejected on the surface of the earth where they cool so rapidly that no crystals form. Exceptionally fast cooling or chilling of molten masses, moreover, forms volcanic glass or obsidian. It is by the application of this same principle that crystal forming is prevented in the manufacture of common glass.

The large size of the crystals forming the granite that fills cracks and fissures of the Inner Gorge at Grand Canyon indicates the considerable depth at which it was formed and is further evidence of the great mountains that existed in this region during the first era in geologic history.

CHAPTER II
THE ALGONKIAN ERA

TILTED ROCKS OF THE SECOND ERA. GRAND CANYON

Rocks formed during the second great era of the earth's history are distinctive in several respects. They are not highly altered or completely changed in form and structure as are those of the oldest era, but are largely free from such changes and, for the most part, similar to rocks which are seen in the process of formation today. Furthermore, they are known to contain definite traces of plant life, though no certain forms of animal life have yet been found in them. They represent a period probably as great as all of subsequent time.

ALGONKIAN ROCKS IN GRAND CANYON

Along Bright Angel Canyon and in several other places in the Grand Canyon, rocks of Algonkian age, representing accumulations of sediments several thousand feet in thickness, are found. Below and to the north of Desert View (southeast of Cape Royal on the North Rim) they form the open floor of the Canyon. Everywhere the most conspicuous layer of this series is a mud rock of brilliant vermilion color. However, the rocks also include a conglomerate or pebble layer, a dark limestone formed principally by plants, and a purple quartzite made by the consolidation of the grains of a sandstone.

FORMATION OF MOUNTAINS (THE ALGONKIAN ERA)

The Algonkian rocks of the Grand Canyon region were bent and broken into mountains at an early date. In many places sloping layers showing the steep angle at which they were tilted are easily visible, even from the Canyon rim. Folded areas and strata which have been shattered are also conspicuous features here and there. The mountains which they formed, however, are now missing for they were worn away in large measure by slow erosion. Today only remnants—small hills on a general level surface—remain in the lower parts of Grand Canyon to tell the story.

EARLY CLIMATES (THE ALGONKIAN ERA)

The rocks of Algonkian age are roughly estimated to be at least six or seven hundred million years old, yet from all indications they were formed under conditions of climate not unlike those of far later periods of history. In several parts of the world traces of great ice sheets—glaciers which scratched and eroded the surface—are found preserved in Algonkian rocks. In other places, including the Grand Canyon, ancient flows of lava are found where they gushed out upon the surface of an old land mass. Among the rocks below Desert View (Navajo) Point and bordering on the Colorado River may readily be seen several black cliffs formed by the volcanic activity of this early age.

The brilliant red shales of Algonkian age found in the lower parts of the Grand Canyon were formed as muds, accumulated probably by large rivers. In these muds are found preserved great quantities of ripple marks, indications of changing currents, also the moulds of salt crystals, and large shrinkage cracks resulting from a very hot sun. In brief, these criteria point toward a hot and probably arid climate in this region during that chapter of history.

OLDEST KNOWN LIFE (THE ALGONKIAN ERA)

The oldest forms of life represented in rocks of Grand Canyon are found in strata of the Second, or Algonkian, Era. Certain layers of limestone showing peculiar structural patterns on their surfaces are interpreted as being the reefs built up through the activities of primitive one-celled plants known as algae. Similar structures are being formed today by plants of this type. Near Harper's Ferry, West Virginia, for example, algae are building up limestone layers almost identical to the fossil ones found in the Algonkian rocks of Grand Canyon. In this connection, it is interesting to note that because of this similarity of the present to the past, the reality of the ancient plant structures was recognized a few years ago. They were discovered at a place in the Grand Canyon just west of the mouth of Bright Angel Creek.

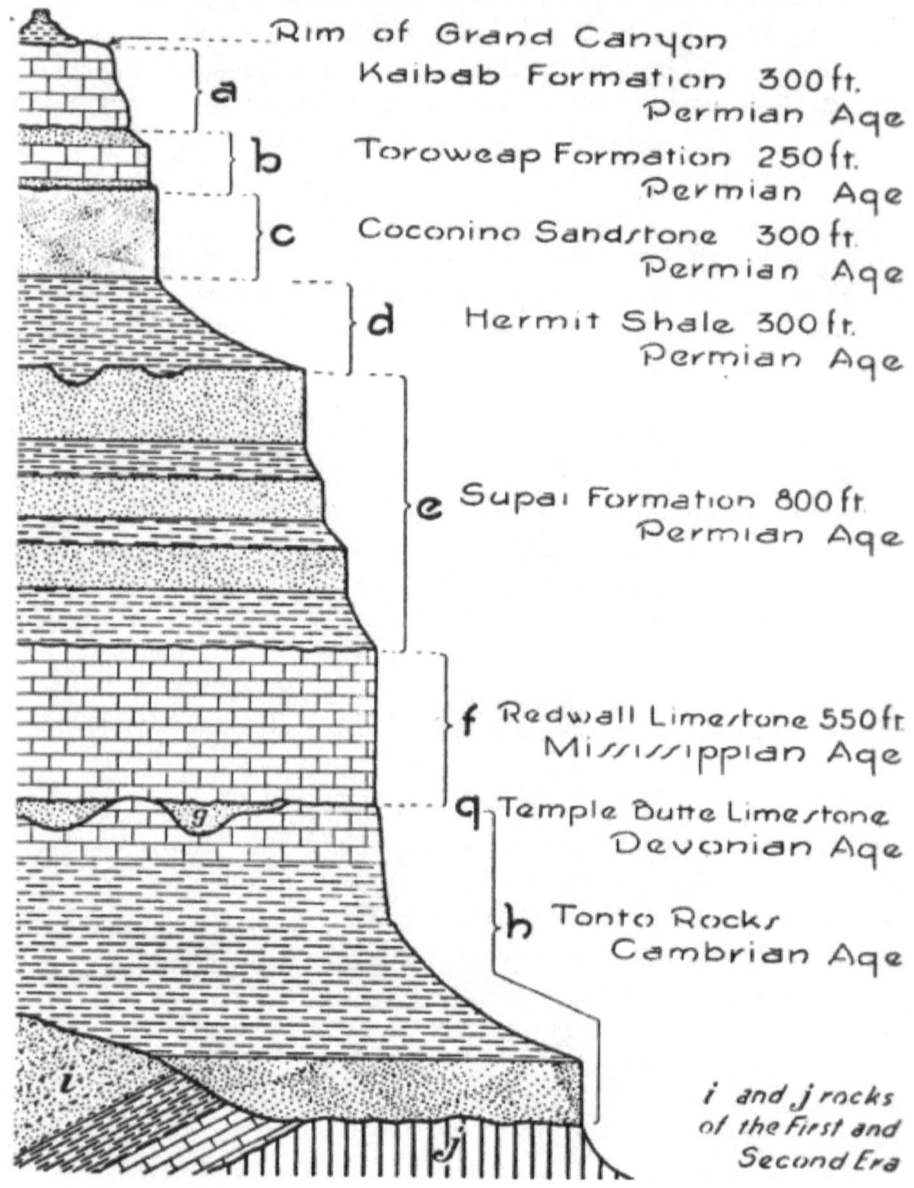

ROCKS OF THE THIRD ERA IN THE GRAND CANYON

Rocks of the Fourth Era (Red Butte)

Rim of Grand Canyon

a~ Sandy limestone formed beneath the sea. In it are found corals, sponges, sharks' teeth and many sea shells.

Kaibab Formation 300 ft.   Permian Age

b~ Red sandstone and gray limestone. Formed at bottom of a shallow sea.

Toroweap Formation 250 ft. Permian Age

c~ Wind-blown sand which was piled in dunes. Contains the tracks of many kinds of primitive reptiles or amphibians.

Coconino Sandstone 300 ft. Permian Age

d~ River mud in which are preserved many impressions of ferns and cone-bearing plants, insect wings, raindrop pits and tracks of salamander-like animals.

Hermit Shale 300 ft. Permian Age

e~ Ancient flood-plain deposits of sand and mud containing impressions of fern-like plants and tracks of land animals.

Supai Formation 800 ft. Permian Age

f~ Sea deposits containing remains of shells, fish, sea-lillies and related forms of life.

Redwall Limestone 550 ft. Mississippian Age

g~ Accumulations of sandy lime in which are preserved the remains of some of the earliest fish.

Temple Butte Limestone Devonian Age

h~ Sand, muds, and limes representing ancient beach which was gradually covered with water until finally the sediments were at a considerable depth beneath the sea. The earliest definite traces of animal life in the canyon found here.

Tonto Rocks Cambrian Age

i and j rocks of the First and Second Era

CHAPTER III
THE PALEOZOIC ERA

It was during the third or middle chapter in the earth's history that all of the apparently horizontal, upper layers in the Grand Canyon walls were formed. As will be seen in the succeeding pages, some of these rocks are sandstones formed from the sands of early beaches or sand dune areas, others are shales—the hardened muds of ancient river deltas—and still others are limestones built up by accumulations of plant and animal remains on sea bottoms. All are rocks formed by the deposition of sediments by wind and water during vast intervals of time. In them have been hidden and preserved many forms of life. Seashells, footprints, fern impressions, and various other traces of early plants and animals remain to tell the story of these ancient times. It is of special interest to note that in rocks formed during the earliest part of this chapter are found the first definite traces of animal life, that in other rocks of this chapter have been found evidences of primitive fish, and that in the most recent rocks of this group occur the traces of early reptiles, insects, ferns, and cone-bearing plants. In the walls of Grand Canyon examples of all of these fossils have been found, and these will be described in detail in the succeeding pages.

FIRST ANIMAL LIFE—THE TONTO ROCKS (CAMBRIAN PERIOD)

Great highlands which were formed in the Grand Canyon region during the Second Era of history were afterwards gradually worn away by erosion until near the start of the next era a flat, almost featureless plain existed. Here and there, however, isolated hills of dark, crystalline rocks of the First Era stood above the general surface, as seen opposite Yaki point. In other places, such as to the west of where Bright Angel Creek now flows, small mountains of red Algonkian rocks (Second Era) remained. Around and against these, sediments were then deposited. Pebbles and sands accumulated, forming a thick layer which today appears as the brown sandstone rim of the Inner Gorge. These represent the first deposits of the Third Era. But the sea was encroaching upon the land during this period, and gradually the sand deposited near shore was covered by mud and this in turn by lime far out from the beach. Today this series of sand, mud and lime is found represented in the rocks of the Tonto Platform in Grand Canyon.

SCENE ON CAMBRIAN SEA FLOOR IN GRAND CANYON REGION
(RECONSTRUCTION. MUSEUM NORTHERN ARIZONA)

Along the Tonto Trail a few hundred yards east of Indian Gardens numerous primitive sea animals have been found buried and preserved in layers of thin shale. Many of these are creatures with rounded shells smaller than the nail of a person's little finger, others are animals related to the snail, and still others are crab-like creatures known as trilobites. The trilobites undoubtedly were the rulers of that age for they excelled not only in numbers but in size. Some specimens from Grand Canyon have measured over three inches in length. Despite this size, however, the trilobites and their associates from the Tonto Platform represent some of the earliest known forms of animal life.

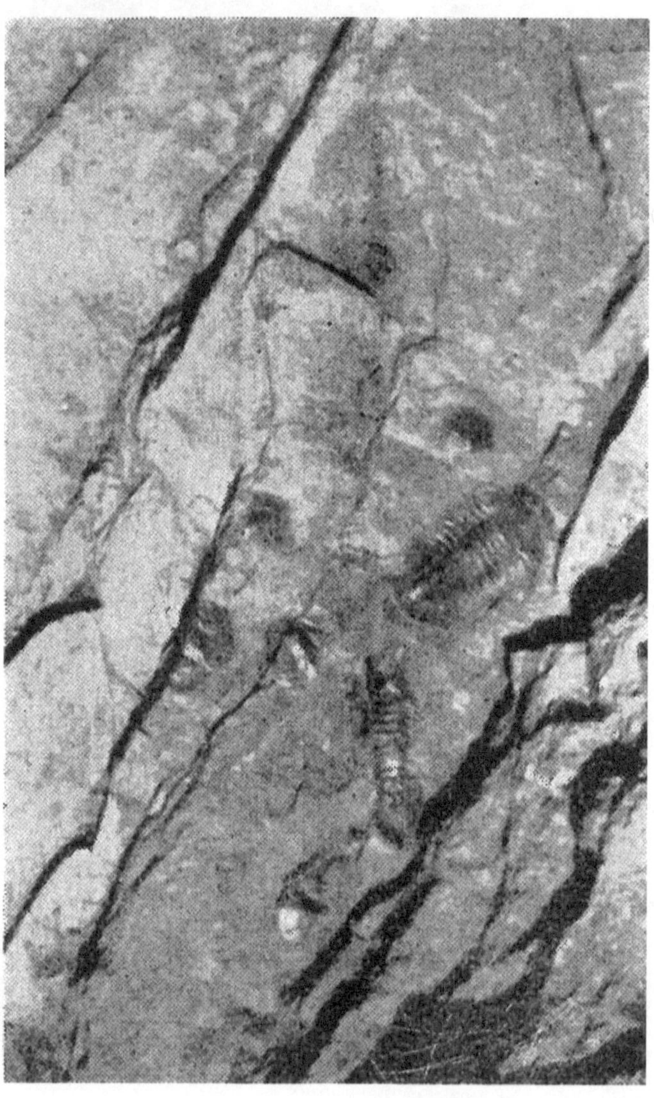

TRILOBITES PRESERVED IN GREEN SHALE OF GRAND CANYON WALLS
(ONE-EIGHTH NATURAL SIZE)

THE MISSING PERIODS OF THE THIRD ERA (ORDOVICIAN AND SILURIAN PERIODS)

The geologist has found that two long periods of history are lacking in the great succession of ages represented by the strata in the Grand Canyon walls. These missing periods which belong to the Third Era are known as the Ordovician, the time when fish first appeared in the seas, and the Silurian, the time when millipeds and scorpions became our first air breathers. These ages immediately followed the Cambrian and involved millions of years. The absence of the first of them is explained by some geologists as the result of its rocks having been completely worn away at a later time. It seems more probable, however, that the Grand Canyon region was above sea level during these two ages so that no sediments were accumulated and consequently no rocks formed.

THE AGE OF FISH (DEVONIAN PERIOD)

A FRESH WATER FISH OF DEVONIAN AGE

During that period of geologic time commonly known as the "age of fish," sands and limes were accumulated on the surface of the Grand Canyon region filling in old river channels and burying the bodies of fish and other animals. The deposits formed at this time were later eroded to a large extent. The surface of the land was worn and washed away until finally only isolated patches or pockets of limestone and sandstone remained. These we find today exposed in the walls of the Grand Canyon occurring just at the base of the great Redwall cliff in about fifteen different localities.

Although fish were rulers of the age during Devonian times, they were of primitive types and apparently depended for defense upon bony skin armour rather than upon speed. The plates and scales of fresh-water fish have been found preserved in the lavender rocks of this age in the Grand Canyon.

SEA LIFE FROM THE NORTH—THE REDWALL LIMESTONE (MISSISSIPPIAN OR LOWER CARBONIFEROUS PERIOD)

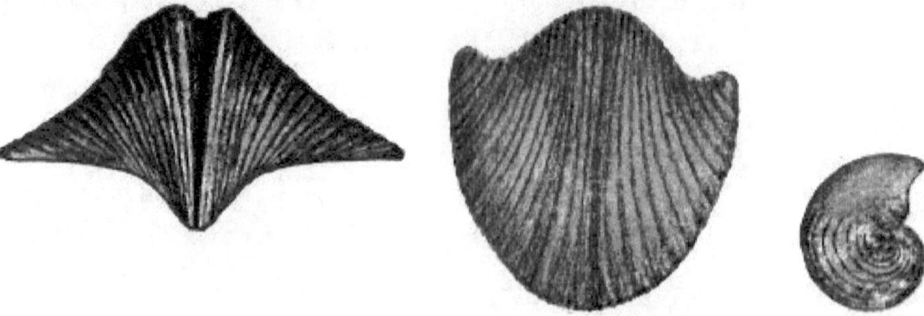

REDWALL FOSSILS (NATURAL SIZE)

One of the most prominent and conspicuous features of the Grand Canyon is the great red cliff of limestone about midway in its walls. This cliff is the highest in the Canyon—averaging about 550 feet in the area of Bright Angel Canyon. In most places it is almost vertical, and in some it even overhangs to such an extent that a visitor once aptly said, "The Washington Monument might be placed beneath it and kept out of the rain."

To the prospector this formation is known as the Blue Lime; to the geologist it is the Redwall Limestone. Both are correct. Actually the rock is a rather pure limestone of a grey or bluish color, but in most places where seen, its surface has been stained a bright red by iron oxides from above. It appears throughout the Grand Canyon as a wide band or ribbon of red.

HAVASU FALLS IN REDWALL LIMESTONE. GRAND CANYON

Large amphitheaters, many curving alcoves, caves, and solution tunnels are all characteristic features of the great Redwall. It is composed of relatively pure lime so rain and other waters have a chemical action upon it—they leach and dissolve it. Waters all tend to drain toward curving centers, and so increase this curving. Everywhere the rounding off of corners takes place.

The origin of the Redwall Limestone is as interesting as its form. The purity of the lime indicates that it was built up in a relatively wide and quiet sea. Its composition represents a vast accumulation of the skeletons of ancient plants and animals. Seashells are found in great numbers, some of them preserved in delicate detail. These and other forms of ocean life clearly indicate that a great sea connection then existed between this region and that of western Canada to the north.

TRACKS IN THE SUPAI SANDSTONE (PERMIAN PERIOD)

During that period in geological history known as the Permian, when some of the beds of soft coal in eastern America were being formed, a large area in northern Arizona was receiving red sediments from the east, probably carried by rivers from the granitic highlands of that region. Today these sediments appear in the Grand Canyon walls as alternating layers of red sandstone and shale immediately above the great Redwall. They are almost a thousand feet in thickness.

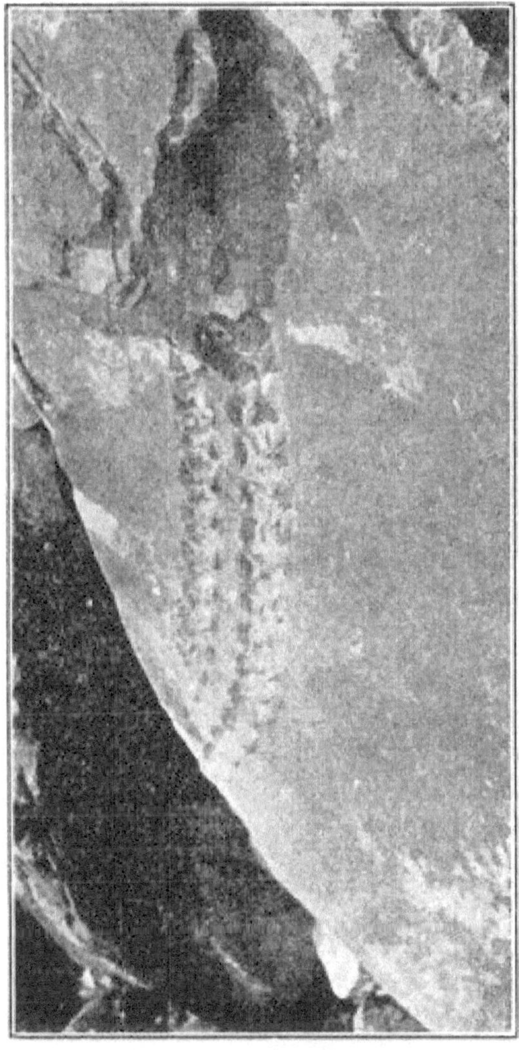

**TRACKS OF SHORT-LEGGED PREHISTORIC ANIMAL. SUPAI FORMA-
TION. GRAND CANYON**

When the red beds were accumulating in this region, the climate probably
was more or less arid; the vegetation consisted principally of ferns and other low-
ly plants; and the animal life included a group of large but primitive four-footed
creatures. Numerous tracks of the latter, preserved in the walls of Grand Canyon,
have provided one of the most interesting discoveries of recent years. Some of
these footprints are several inches in length, and the number of toes varies between three and five. They show no close relationship to the tracks of other localities, and apparently represent a fauna new to North America.

LANDSCAPES OF THE HERMIT SHALE (PERMIAN PERIOD)

LANDSCAPE AT TIME HERMIT SHALE WAS FORMING
(RECONSTRUCTION. MUSEUM NORTHERN ARIZONA)

FOSSIL FERN FROM THE HERMIT SHALE (REDUCED)

Concerning the conditions under which the topmost red formation of the Grand Canyon (the Hermit Shale) was developed, and the nature of its origin, we have today a rather definite and interesting picture. A wealth of fossil plants and a number of tracks of animals have been found excellently preserved in its muddy layers, and by means of these and other indications the following conclusions have been drawn.

The Hermit Shale represents accumulations of mud and fine sandy material deposited probably by streams flowing from the northeast. Here and there are found evidences of pools and arroyos with wavy ripple marks on their borders. and a thin film of shiny slime covering the surface. The trails of worms, the footprints of small salamander-like animals, and the fronds of ferns, mostly mascerated or wilted, are found delicately preserved in this slime. Raindrop impressions, the molds of salt crystals and numerous sun-cracks also add to the picture. This region has been described by Dr. David White as "the scene of showers, burning sun, hailstorms, occasional torrents and periods of drought and drying up of pools" during Hermit times.

Thirty-five species of plants are at present known from the Hermit Shale of Grand Canyon. Many of these have not been found elsewhere in the world, though some were representatives of European plants, and others had their closest relations in central Asia, India, Australia, Africa, and South America. This fossil flora consists principally of ferns and small cone-bearing plants, all of which were relatively dwarfed in size and appear less dense than those of corresponding age found in eastern America. They apparently indicate a semi-arid climate with long dry seasons, for the absence of moist-climate and swamp-loving types is noticeable.

Several insect wings have been found in the Hermit Shale, one of which was four inches in length. Numerous footprints of vertebrate animals have also been found, and undoubtedly represent an interesting fauna.

WIND-BLOWN SAND—THE COCONINO (PERMIAN PERIOD)

The light-colored formation which appears as a conspicuous ribbon-like band around the upper part of the Grand Canyon has long presented a puzzle concerning its origin. The grains of white sand of which it is composed apparently were deposited at steep angles, for the many and varied slopes which were formed may be readily seen today on the surface of the rock. These slopes were probably once the lee sides of sand dunes deposited by winds in an area bordering the sea. We find the only traces of life in this formation represented by the trails of ancient worms and insects, and by the foot-prints of early lizard, or salamander-like creatures. Already the tracks of some 27 species of animals have been discovered in this sandstone within the Grand Canyon, though strangely enough no bones have yet been located.

WIND-BLOWN SAND. COCONINO FORMATION. GRAND CANYON

TRACKS OF PRIMITIVE FOUR-FOOTED ANIMALS, COCONINO SAND-STONE. GRAND CANYON

PHOTO BY E. W. ENSOR

WARM SEAS FROM THE WEST—THE TOROWEAP AND KAIBAB FORMATIONS (PERMIAN PERIOD)

SEASHELLS FROM KAIBAB LIMESTONE (REDUCED)

Along both sides of Grand Canyon at the top, two buff and gray layers of limestone stand out as massive cliffs separated by a tree-covered slope. The upper of these limestones forms the plateau surface and may be seen for a great distance in every direction. Both layers were formed as the result of vast accumulations of organic and sandy materials on sea bottoms, and in places are composed largely of the remains of marine life—shells, corals and sponges. The teeth of sharks have also been found in the upper limestone.

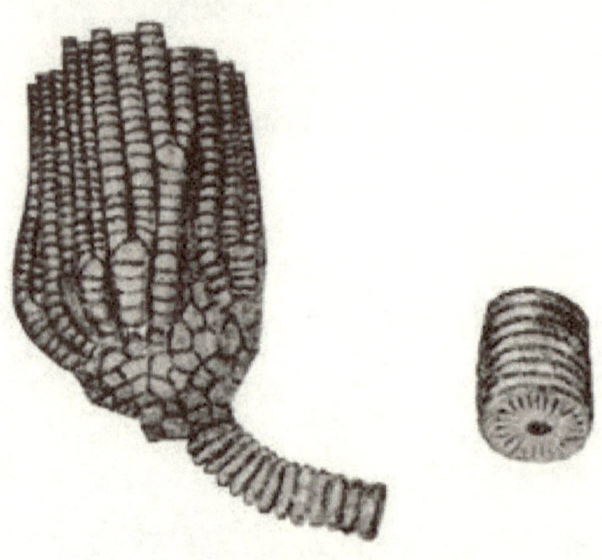

SEA LILY OR CRINOID (REDUCED)

HORN CORAL (NATURAL SIZE)

During the early stages of the period when these marine animals lived and multiplied in the region, a great body of salt water extended over its surface from far to the west, remained briefly, then retreated from the area. Soon, however, marine waters advanced once more and another sea was formed with its shoreline extending eastward even beyond the region in which we now find Grand Canyon. Evidences of the second and larger sea are found beyond Flagstaff to the south, in the Painted Desert to the east, and almost to Zion Canyon to the north.

The presence of corals and sharks' teeth not only indicates that this region was covered on more than one occasion by marine waters, but also suggests that these seas were warm and shallow. This is estimated to have been some 200 million years ago.

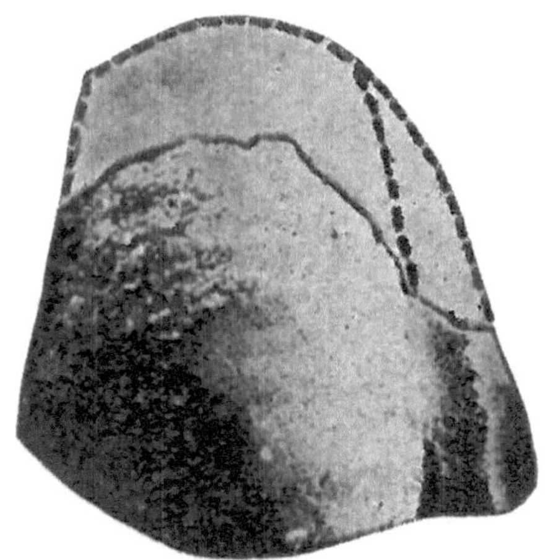

FOSSIL SHARK'S TOOTH (NATURAL SIZE)

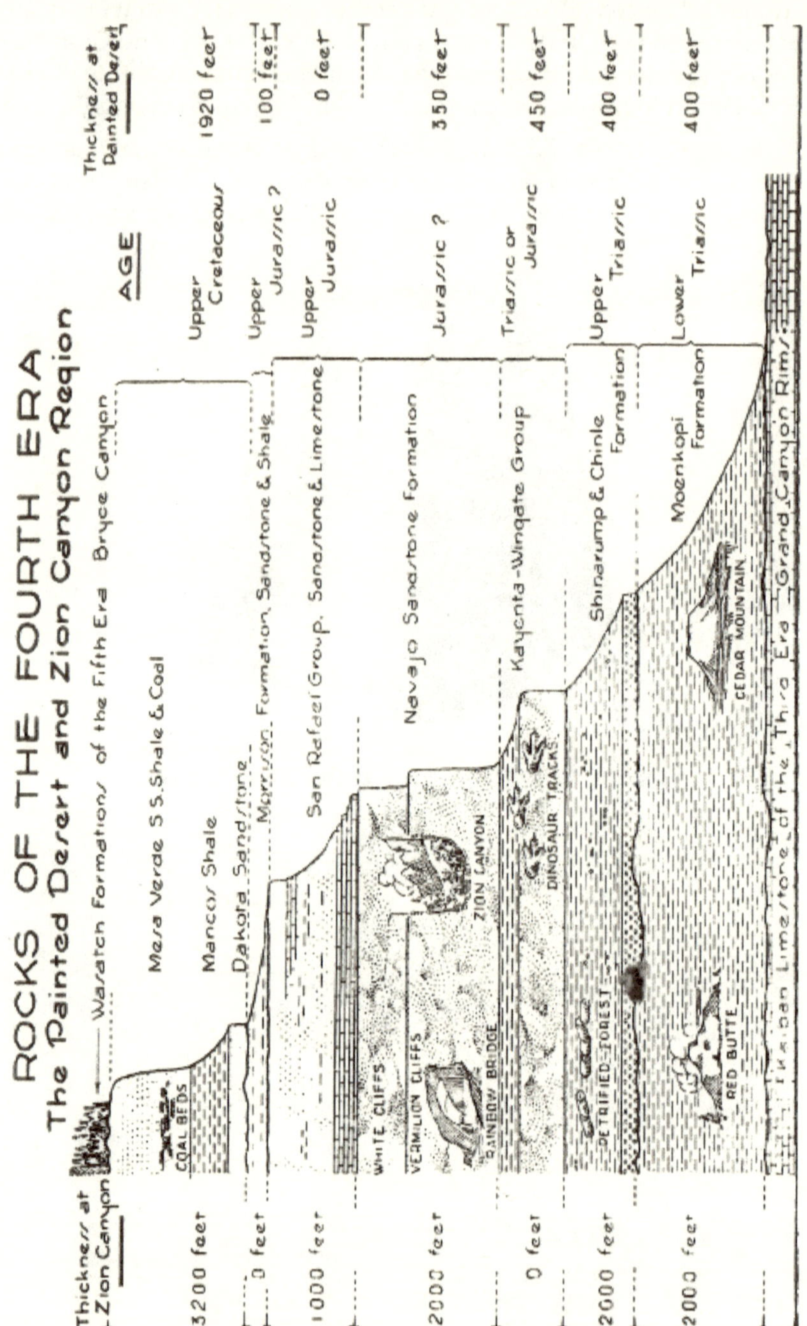

ROCKS OF THE FOURTH ERA

The Painted Desert and Zion Canyon Region

CHAPTER IV

THE MESOZOIC ERA

The Fourth Chapter of the earth's history is commonly known as "the age of dinosaurs." Large reptiles were the dominating forms of life all over the world during this age. Landscapes and types of climate varied considerably, and in the Grand Canyon region they changed completely several times. During some periods ocean bodies covered the country; at others desert winds piled up dunes on the surface. Again this region was the flood plain of rivers, where pebbles, mud and great logs of pine were washed in and deposited. At still other times coal was formed in some quantity. All of these interesting features of the Fourth Chapter will be briefly treated in the pages following. Their records as found at Zion Canyon to the north, in the Painted Desert to the east, and at the Petrified Forest to the south are such that a visitor to the region can scarcely help but marvel and wonder at their meaning.

REMNANTS OF YOUNGER STRATA—RED BUTTE AND CEDAR MOUNTAIN (MOENKOPI FORMATION: TRIASSIC PERIOD)

Two isolated hills of unusual interest rise above the plateau surface near Grand Canyon. Looking east from Desert View (Navajo) Point one of these, a flat-topped mesa called Cedar Mountain, may be seen. The other, known as Red Butte, is a rounded hill about fifteen miles to the south of Grand Canyon village. The most interesting feature of these hills is found in the fact that they are composed for the most part of red sandstones and shales which once formed a continuous layer over this entire plateau region. These same rocks are found throughout southern Utah to the north, and in the Painted Desert to the east. Except at Red Butte and Cedar Mountain they have been completely stripped off and eroded away from the vicinity of Grand Canyon. The time involved in this erosion was tremendous and the consequences widespread. As a result the present flat plateau surface was formed—a great plain high above sea level. The persistence of Red Butte and Cedar Mountain against time and the elements is easily explained, moreover, by the hard lava cap of the former and the protecting layer of pebble-rock on top of the latter.

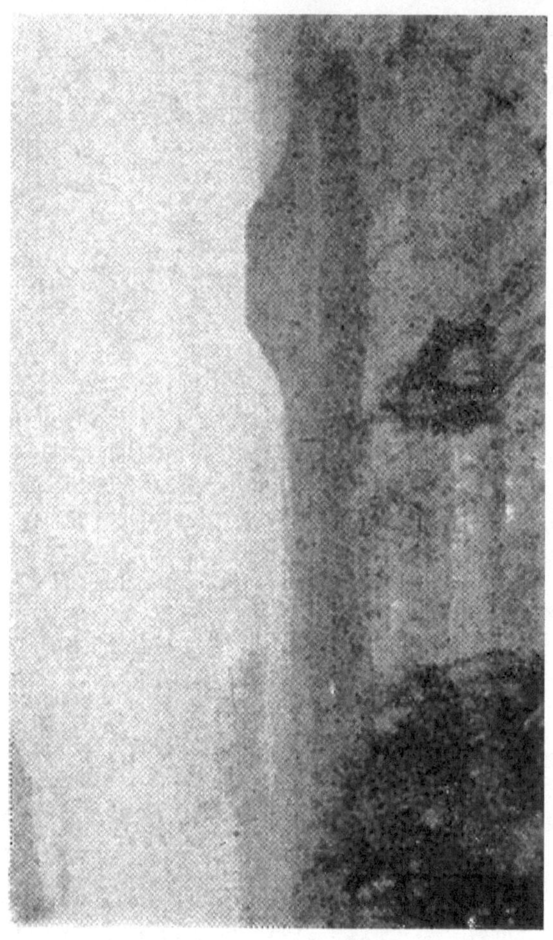

CEDAR MOUNTAIN

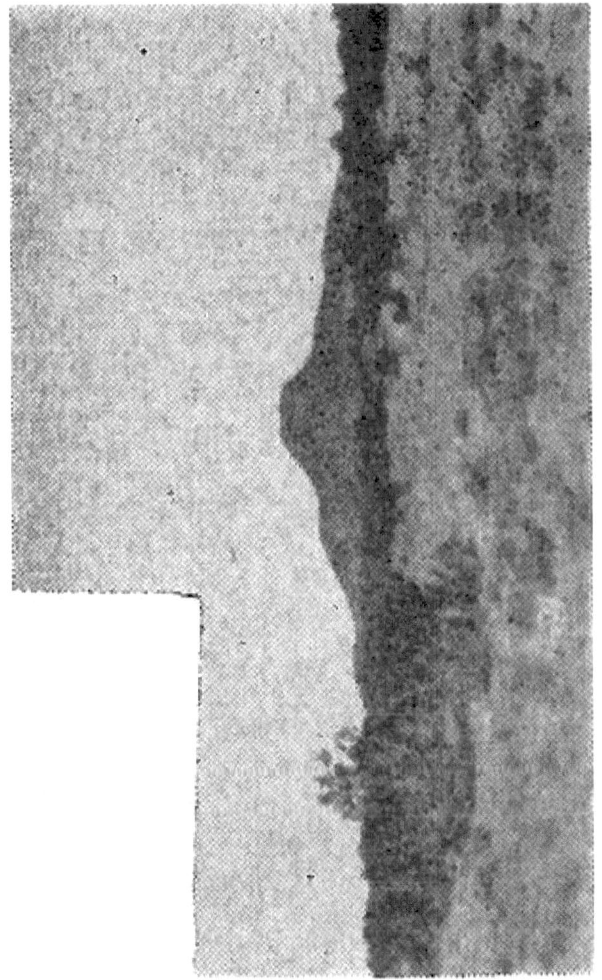

RED BUTTE

The red sandstones and shales found in Red Butte and Cedar Mountain were formed from sands and muds accumulated during the early part of the Triassic Age—the beginning of the fourth great era of history. Near Flagstaff at the southernmost limit of the formation have been found many tracks and trails left by small crawling animals which indicate a shore environment in that section. In the same formation found in Utah and other places to the north are many seashells of various types. Gypsum, an indication of arid climate, is also found to a large extent in the rocks of this group.

THE PETRIFIED FOREST (SHINARUMP AND CHINLE FORMATIONS; TRIASSIC PERIOD)

The Petrified Forests of northern Arizona and southern Utah were formed from trees which grew during a period known as the Triassic. The type of environment in the Painted Desert region during that period makes a very interesting speculation. The landscape of this ancient country, as interpreted from the present rock formations found there, was that of a low, flat area, perhaps a floodplain, where rivers and streams meandered back and forth, depositing first large pebbles and sand, and later a great thickness of finer material consisting of sand and much mud. It was by these streams that a great quantity of logs of evergreen trees was carried down probably from mountains to the south or southwest. Many of the tree trunks were worn and battered on the way, and in this region (from southern Utah to the vicinity of Adamana and Holbrook) they were buried in great numbers among the depositing sediments. All four of the Petrified Forests south of Adamana originated in this manner—and probably represent old log-jams. Nine miles north of Adamana, however, is the North Sigillaria Forest where the trees are found standing as they grew.

PETRIFIED FOREST. ARIZONA

PETRIFIED LOGS OF TRIASSIC AGE

A large majority of the fossil trees in Petrified Forest National Monument represent a pine-like species belonging to a group now extinct in the northern hemisphere. Some individuals of this type have diameters as great as ten feet and heights of more than 200 feet. Four or five other varieties of tree occur but they are less common and rather inconspicuous.

The process by which these trees were changed to stone took place a very long time after they were buried beneath sands and silts. At a time probably millions of years later, waters bearing in solution the mineral silica passed through the rocks of this region. Particle by particle wood was decayed, and almost simultaneously it was replaced by silica. The brilliant colors found in much of it are due to small quantities of iron and manganese which were introduced in a similar manner.

The wicked-looking upper jaw of a phytosaur—relative of the crocodile—has been discovered buried in one of the colorful mounds of mud out in the Petrified Forest. In nearby deposits are found still other fossils including ferns preserved in delicate detail and clamlike shells. These, together with the petrified logs of evergreen trees, make the picture very much alive and real to one whose imagination allows him to review these fascinating early pages in history.

DINOSAUR TRACKS (WINGATE-KAYENTA; JURASSIC PERIOD)

Dinosaur means "terrible lizard." Everyone has heard this name and attaches to it at least a vague conception of a creature of peculiar shape and tremendous size. In the dim far-away past these giant reptiles lived, developed and died in many parts of this country, but to most of us, they are only fantastic creatures in literature—not live or moving animals.

DINOSAUR TRACKS. PAINTED DESERT

The reality of the dinosaur should become apparent to those who travel through the Painted Desert region of Arizona. In that country the grey and red hills of clay, the cliffs of sand and the many brightly colored layers of hardened mud represent a part of the ancient landscape in which lived the "terrible lizards." Furthermore, life definitely inserts itself into this picture when a person sees in the rocks the very three-toed tracks left by the dinosaur. Who can deny the story of life when he can place his fingers in the foot impressions and measure the strides of these animals—many of them—both large and small? Such is the privilege of those who visit the Painted Desert just south of Tuba City.

The tracks of the dinosaurs are found in rocks which apparently were formed from river deposits of sands and muds. In other rocks closely associated have been found the bones of dinosaurs, other reptiles, and animals related to the frog or toad. Some of these creatures apparently were "largely if not entirely terrestrial in habit" while others probably lived in either fresh water streams or swamps.

THE PAINTED DESERT

THE ROCKS OF ZION CANYON AND RAINBOW NATURAL BRIDGE (NAVAJO SANDSTONE; JURASSIC PERIOD)

The lure of a desert with its drifting sands, its scattered oases, and its broad extent has ever been great. Today in the Southwest, cut off from the moist ocean breezes of the west by the lofty Sierra Nevadas and further isolated by the Rocky

Mountains to the east, is America's great desert region. Here the winds and the rains are constantly at work tearing down and sculpturing the great land masses, while in places the wind is piling up the sand and debris to form dunes and new lands.

Far back in history, probably in what is known as the Jurassic Period, southwestern United States witnessed conditions of climate and environment which were perhaps somewhat comparable though probably far more desert-like than those which exist today. The land which had been raised in the preceding period to form a great flood-plain remained above sea level. Lofty mountains were formed to the west and like the Sierras of today, they robbed the east-travelling winds of their moisture. These mountains were very high and furnished a vast supply of sediment which was carried down into the arid basin to the east, worked and reworked by the wind, and finally deposited as a great layer of sand.

ZION CANYON. NAVAJO SANDSTONE

RAINBOW NATURAL BRIDGE. NAVAJO SANDSTONE

The beautiful Vermilion Cliffs and the White Cliffs of southern Utah which together form the walls of Zion Canyon, the red sandstone out of which is carved Rainbow Natural Bridge, and the jagged Echo Cliffs seen to the northeast of Desert View (Navajo) Point at Grand Canyon are all monuments of the Jurassic Age. These high walls are of sandstone—formed from sand steeply piled at varying angles. They have been aptly called "cliffs of fossil sand dunes."

While desert winds and a burning sun were playing a prominent part in the

Grand Canyon region, during the Jurassic Age, other sections of the country were favored with a moist climate and luxuriant vegetation. Dinosaurs and other reptiles waded about in swamps and developed to tremendous sizes. The country teemed with life, very different from that of today, yet none the less interesting.

FROM SEASHELLS TO COAL BEDS (DAKOTA. MANCOS, MESA VERDE; CRETACEOUS PERIOD)

CRETACEOUS SHELLS FROM SOUTHERN UTAH

During the last part of the "Age of Dinosaurs," in that period of history known as the Cretaceous, much of northeastern Arizona, southern Utah, and northwestern New Mexico apparently was submerged beneath a sea. Mollusks abounded, and various other types of water animals swam or crawled in this region. Their shells were buried and preserved among the muds and limes which were accumulating, and today many of them are found in the rocks of this age.

As time went on, the Cretaceous seas were expelled from their basins in the Southwest. Low-lying coastal plains—two hundred and more miles wide—with luxuriant vegetation and perhaps swamps, replaced them, and these new conditions were the means of much coal formation. Great accumulations of vegetable matter, buried beneath sediments brought down by streams, eventually formed the many layers of coal which today are found in various places in Utah, Arizona, and New Mexico. In the last named state some extensive and valuable coal beds are found in rocks of this age near Gallup. Impressions of leaves and pieces of fossil wood are also numerous among these rocks and they indicate that there was a warm, moist climate during that period in which they grew.

The Cretaceous Period ended with a general change of conditions or a revolution, the world over. Many of the seas were changed into lands, new mountains were formed and the dinosaurs and giant reptiles were largely replaced by mammals and other modern varieties of life.

COAL CANYON. PAINTED DESERT COUNTRY
AERIAL PHOTO COPYRIGHT FRED HARVEY

CHAPTER V

THE CENOZOIC ERA

Although chapter five is the most recent in the earth's history and lasts up to the present day, evidences of its life and its happenings are extremely meager in the Grand Canyon region. With the exceptions of the fresh water deposits formed during the very early part (Bryce Canyon formations) and of the many volcanoes built in the later stages, no rocks were formed here during that chapter. This region was then above sea level and erosion was working continuously. The great level plain which today forms the plateau surface at Grand Canyon was created by the wearing away of overlying rocks. The Grand Canyon itself and also Zion and Bryce Canyons were sculptured. In fact, all of the features of erosion which today make this desert region so picturesque and fanciful owe their origin to the various agents of erosion which have been at work during this most recent chapter of the world's history.

The "Age of Mammals" is a name often applied to the last era. Creatures not unlike some of the most advanced forms of life found today lived even in the early parts of this age. As the era progressed, nevertheless, a development was noticeable until finally in the very last part man himself appeared. Though few remains of this interesting and comparatively recent life have been found in northern Arizona and southern Utah, still a few elephant tusks, some camel teeth and the more recent remains of early cliff and pueblo dwellers give evidence of a thrilling history during parts of this era.

In the following pages will be found brief sketches of some of these interesting features represented in the Grand Canyon region. The many activities of erosion such as canyon-forming, the eruption of volcanoes, influences of the great ice sheets of the north, crustal movements, fragmentary evidences of early mammals, and lastly early man himself are all introduced.

BRYCE CANYON FORMATION (WASATCH: EOCENE EPOCH)

The formation found at Bryce Canyon and at Cedar Breaks in southern Utah has the distinction of being composed of the most recently formed sedimentary rocks in this plateau region. It was during the early part of the last great chapter of history that lime and some sand were accumulating here in fresh water. They are believed by most geologists to represent the deposits of ancient lakes and in them are found freshwater mollusks. Rivers and other agents of deposition probably also took a part in the forming of these strata as is indicated by the great irregularity and variety of sand and other sediments. Truly the origin of these rocks presents an interesting problem.

BRYCE CANYON

AERIAL PHOTO COPYRIGHT FRED HARVEY

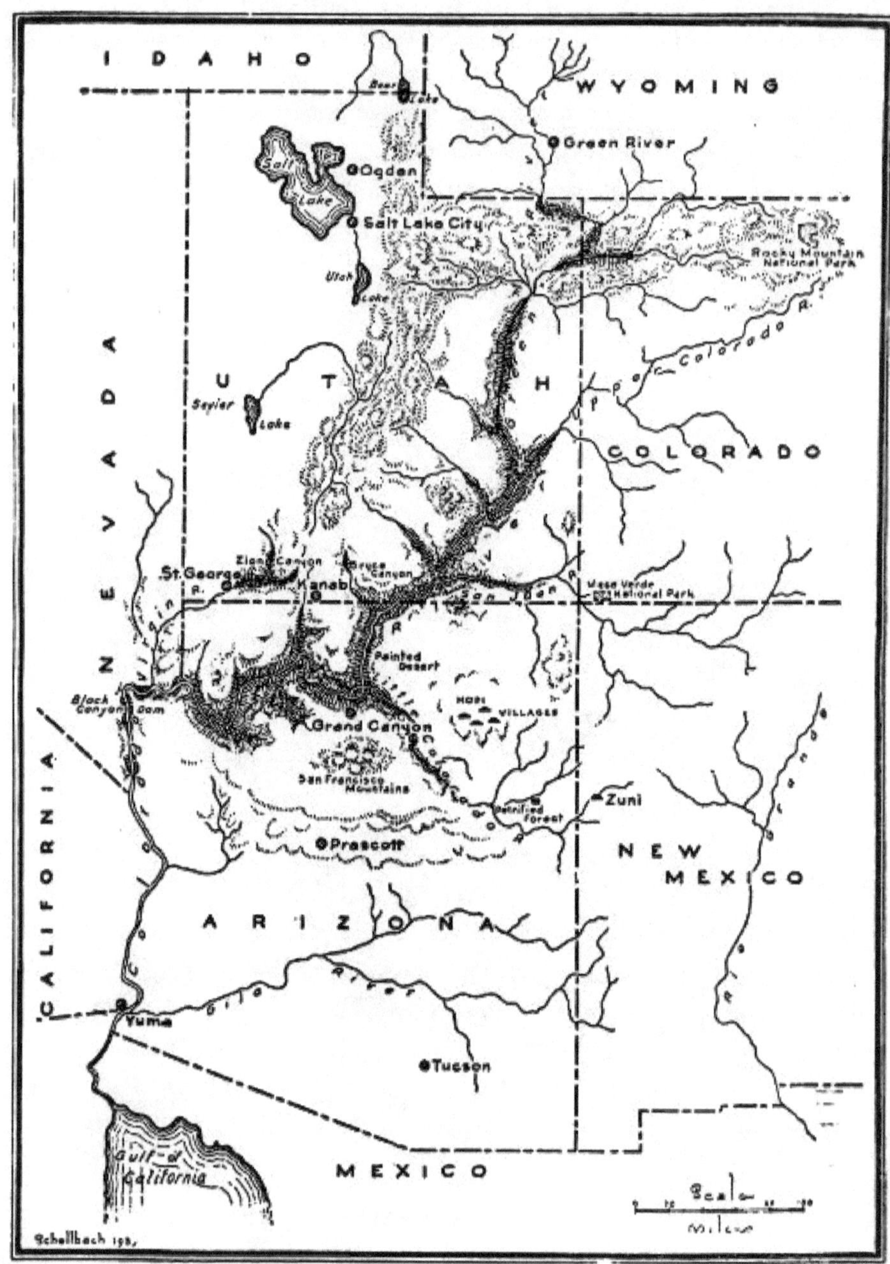

MAP OF THE COLORADO RIVER

The delicate and beautiful colors of Bryce are due to the white limestone which in many places retains its creamy color, but in others has been stained a vivid pink by the drainage from upland washes. The Canyon itself is almost entirely the result of running water which has carved and etched its pattern during geologically recent times. Just as the Grand Canyon and Zion Canyon were made possible by a great elevation of the land in this region, so also was Bryce affected. The small streams of the Paunsagunt Plateau were given power to cut into the sandstones and limestones which form the Pink Cliffs, and due to the peculiar nature of these rocks the many spires, promontories, and pinnacles were formed as remnants of erosion in the valleys.

A GREAT EROSION SURFACE (CENOZOIC AGE)

The level, flat and almost featureless skyline of Grand Canyon is an outstanding characteristic of the plateau of northern Arizona. This surface is fascinating to some; monotonous to others. To all, it is one of the most striking features of the region. The history which it represents, moreover, is of extreme interest and impressive length. Here on the top of the great plateau is seen the result of vast erosion. Long periods of work by water, wind, and other elements have gradually worn away strata that were once above. Just as erosion is forming the Grand Canyon today, so it has accomplished this much greater task. Several thousand feet of materials have been removed from the surface over much of this entire region.

A GREAT EROSION SURFACE

NATIONAL PARK SERVICE

South of Grand Canyon, at Red Butte, east in the Painted Desert, and north in Utah are found remnants of those rocks which once formed a continuous layer over the present plateau. Red sandstones and shales representing former sands and muds of shallow water and beach, pebble-rocks and marls deposited by rivers and containing the remains of cone-bearing trees, crocodiles, and dinosaurs—all these rocks and probably others once gave color to this area just as today they lend brilliance to the Painted Desert and to southern Utah. In those places high cliffs mark the lines of recession—the stages of the constant retreat of the rocks from the Grand Canyon region before ever-working forces of erosion. Red Butte to the south of Grand Canyon, on the other hand, has been preserved as an isolated remnant of the same rocks by its hard, resistant cap of lava. Thus we have mute evidence of a tremendously large and wonderful story of former lands, and of their later wearing away to leave the great plain which now forms the surface of the plateau about Grand Canyon.

CRUSTAL MOVEMENT AT GRAND CANYON (CENOZOIC AGE)

Many visitors to the Grand Canyon are distinctly surprised when they find numerous seashells, corals, and sponges, beautifully preserved in the limestone layer upon which they are standing. The idea immediately occurs that this region was once beneath the sea. Obviously then either the land has risen or the ocean has receded.

A careful study of the region shows that the rock strata which form the great plateau of northern Arizona have been bent into a huge arch or dome. The Santa Fe railway travels steadily up grade to the south rim of Grand Canyon which is 7,000 feet above sea level. The north rim is a thousand feet higher, while fifteen miles farther north a high point of 9,000 feet is attained. In southern Utah the limestone layer which forms the top of Grand Canyon passes beneath the surface at 4,000 feet.

Why crustal movements occur is not definitely known though many theories have been advanced to explain them. It is significant, nevertheless, that such movements have gone on in all parts of the world many times in history, and that in many regions they are taking place today. Parts of the California coast are known to be rising, while some other parts of the country are sinking slowly.

The question of whether or not the Grand Canyon region is still rising today cannot be answered with assuredness, but certain it is that it has been both above and below sea level at many different times in history.

It is the slow sinking of the region which has made possible great accumulations of sediments and the building up of rock layers. It is the rising of the land which has brought about great cycles of erosion such as apparently have occurred several times in the history of the Southwest. Since today this region is high above sea level, erosion is rapid. Not only does this elevation give the Colorado River and its tributaries speed and power to erode downward, but also it gives them unusual depth through which to cut and to carve the canyons which are their valleys. Without the rising of this plateau region, the colossal gorges, the weird, sculptured forms of erosion, all of the fascinating and picturesque features of this region could not be.

CUTTING THE GRAND CANYON (PLIOCENE AND PLEISTO-CENE EPOCHS)

"WHAT FORCE HAS FORMED THIS MASTERPIECE OF AWE?
WHAT HANDS HAVE WROUGHT THESE WONDERS IN THE WASTE?
O RIVER, GLEAMING IN THE NARROW RIFT
OF GLOOM THAT CLEAVES THE VALLEY'S NETHER DEEP,
FIERCE COLORADO, PRISONED BY THY TOIL,
AND BLINDLY TOILING STILL TO REACH THE SEA.
THY WATERS, GATHERED FROM THE SNOWS AND SPRINGS
AMID THE UTAH HILLS, HAVE CARVED THIS ROAD
OF GLORY TO THE CALIFORNIA GULF."

—HENRY VAN DYKE

Very difficult is it for the average human fully to realize, to comprehend the tremendous power of running water. One does not question the origin of a wayside gulch cut out by recent storms, nor is it hard to visualize the formation of some steep-walled glen where a fast-rushing stream is found at work in its bottom. The vast Grand Canyon, however, an extreme example of erosion, seems a bit too large—too wide and deep—to be attributed alone to the power of any river such as exists today. But the Grand Canyon—the greatest of chasms—is nothing more than the result of the work of running water over a long period of history.

DIAGRAMMATIC CROSS SECTIONS OF GRAND CANYON

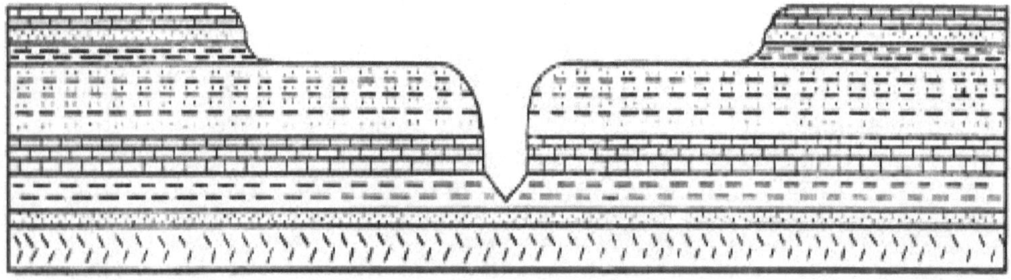

NEAR THE WESTERN END OF NATIONAL PARK. ROCKS OF THE THIRD ERA ALONE HERE FORM THE CANYON WALLS. THOSE OF THE FIRST ERA ARE PROBABLY NOT FAR BELOW THE RIVER BED.

CENTRAL OR BRIGHT ANGEL AREA. THE INNER GORGE IS CUT IN HARD VERTICAL ROCKS OF THE FIRST ERA (ARCHEAN). THE UPPER CANYON WALLS ARE FORMED OF HORIZONTAL ROCKS OF THE THIRD ERA. THE TILTED STRATA OF THE SECOND ERA WERE HERE WORN AWAY EXCEPT TO THE LEFT OF THE GORGE.

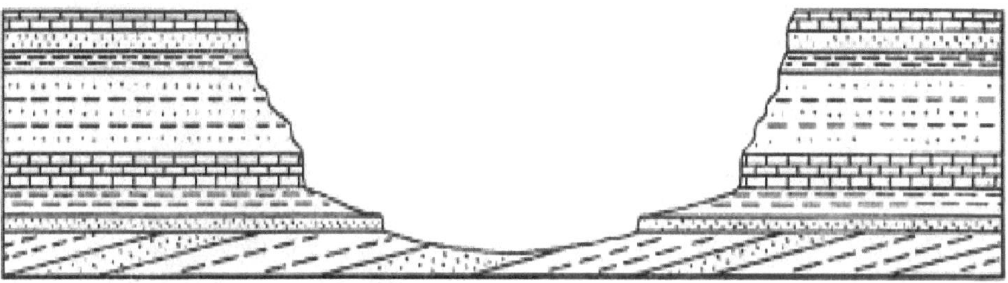

EASTERN END (DESERT VIEW, CAPE ROYAL). THE FLOOR OF THE CANYON IS HERE FORMED OF TILTED ROCKS OF THE SECOND ERA. THE UPPER WALLS ARE OF COMPARATIVELY HORIZONTAL ROCKS OF THE THIRD ERA.

THE GRAND CANYON

Those who have been to the rocky shores of the Colorado River in Grand Canyon, who have heard its wild roar, and seen its mad waves rush along their course, need no further introduction to the power of this stream. It is a mighty river! In the open stretch above the mouth of Bright Angel Creek its speed varies between two and a half and ten miles an hour. Its width at the same place is over one hundred yards and its depth between twelve and forty-five feet. But the Colorado River alone would have made but little progress were it not for the many rocks—boulders, pebbles, and sand grains—all of which act as tools and are constantly gouging and cutting as they move. Just as sandpaper rubbing over the same place continuously leaves its groove, so this combination of power and tools is ever carving its course. The Colorado River during a vast period has cut almost a mile vertically through all of the great rock layers now exposed in the walls of Grand Canyon.

The width of the Grand Canyon, an average of about ten miles, has been brought about by the wearing and washing-in of its sides by natural processes of erosion. Rain, wind, frost, temperature changes and plant action have all combined to break down the Canyon walls. The soft rocks on the slopes are continually being broken and removed; the more resistant ones in the cliffs are undermined so in time fall down. While the river has been cutting deeper, the Canyon's sides have been steadily receding. The Grand Canyon itself is the valley of the Colorado, and its narrowness rather than its width is the remarkable feature when compared with the valleys of other rivers. This present canyon profile has been brought about as the combined effects of an arid climate and a rapidly downward cutting river.

Even a distant view of the Colorado River in the Grand Canyon bottom is sufficient to convince one of the tremendous transporting power of this stream. Thus it not only does the work of cutting downward, but also carries off the vast load of sand and silt which is continually emptied into its waters. It has been aptly described as being "too thick to drink but too thin to plow." In this region the river known at its headwaters as the "Silvery Colorado" bears even a higher percentage of sediment than does the muddy Mississippi-Missouri. It has been found from carefully made tests by the United States Geological Survey that the Colorado River carries past any given point in the Grand Canyon an average of nearly a million tons of sand and silt every day. Thus has the Grand Canyon been excavated!

THE FORMING OF ZION CANYON (PLIOCENE AND PLEISTOCENE EPOCHS)

"A Yosemite Valley in colors" is a very apt description which has often been applied to Zion Canyon in southern Utah. Sheer-walled with a beautiful flat valley floor, this canyon is not unlike California's glacier-carved fairyland in general size and shape, but in formation it has a very different history.

ZION CANYON

The brilliant Vermilion Cliffs which form the bottom two thousand feet of Zion's walls and the contrasting White Cliffs which rise an additional thousand feet are hard, resistant sandstones. Wherever these rocks are found, they form conspicuous perpendicular cliffs because of their hardness, yet even they show the results of the constant attacks of weather and erosion over long periods. From once continuous layers, they have in many places gradually been cut and dissected by running water until now numerous canyons expose their secrets.

It was relatively late in the last chapter of the earth's history (Cenozoic Era) that the cutting of Zion and associated canyons was made possible by gradual though tremendous crustal movements in the region. The then broad, low-lying country was raised several thousand feet to about its present altitude. This was the means of giving power to the streams, including the masterstream — the Virgin River. Steadily and relentlessly these active agents of erosion, heavy-laden with their tools, the muds, sands, and pebbles, have been cutting notches and then canyons. Zion Creek itself, which is one of the largest tributaries of the Virgin River, has cut downward through all of the layers now exposed in the walls of its canyon, and the rock fragments derived from these have been the means of grinding and gouging. As the stream has struggled in its course, these sides have slowly but surely receded through the combined efforts of rain, wind, frost and plants. They have been undermined and otherwise attacked, but as yet represent comparatively little progress in widening. Beautiful Zion Canyon, therefore, has been created as the result of crustal movements bringing into action the effective cutting power of running water, assisted by all the ever-working forces of disintegration and decay.

GLACIERS (PLEISTOCENE EPOCH)

"What part did glaciers play in cutting the Grand Canyon?" This is a question asked almost daily on the rim of that great chasm. Everyone has heard of the mighty ice sheets which somewhere back in geologic history covered a large part of eastern and midwestern United States. Many people have seen beautiful Yosemite Valley in the far west, and have been told how it was carved by the action of glaciers. It is not altogether strange, therefore, that visitors to the Grand Canyon should associate the cutting power of ice with that tremendous gash in the earth's surface. But geologists agree that the glaciers of the Ice Ages had no direct part in the story of Grand Canyon. No scratches or gouges made by ice are to be found on the canyon walls, no great rock piles formed at a glacier's front are in evidence, and lastly, the very V-shape of the canyon itself is vastly different from the usual flat-bottomed valley scooped out by moving ice.

During the last epoch of geologic history, climatic conditions the world over altered very materially. Upon five different occasions snow accumulated in the north to form extensive ice sheets which advanced steadily toward the equator and then retreated with a later change in conditions. These were not the only ice ages in history, but they were of such a comparatively recent date that their influence is strongly felt today in many parts of the world. At the time of greatest expansion the glaciers reached New York in the east, Missouri in the mid west, and Washington in the far west. Contemporaneous with these main ice sheets, furthermore, were large glaciers throughout the Rocky Mountains and the Sierra Nevadas. In the mountains of Utah and even in the San Francisco Peaks, just south of the Grand Canyon, are found evidences of glaciers of this period. Evidently then, climatic conditions in the Southwest as elsewhere were greatly different from those of today. It is believed that there was much more rainfall and less evaporation, as shown by the extensive lakes which existed in this region at that time. Furthermore, the later melting of the glaciers must have supplied a vast quantity of water to the Colorado River causing it to be far larger and more powerful than today.

SAN FRANCISCO MOUNTAIN VOLCANIC FIELD (PLIO-CENE AND PLEISTOCENE EPOCHS)

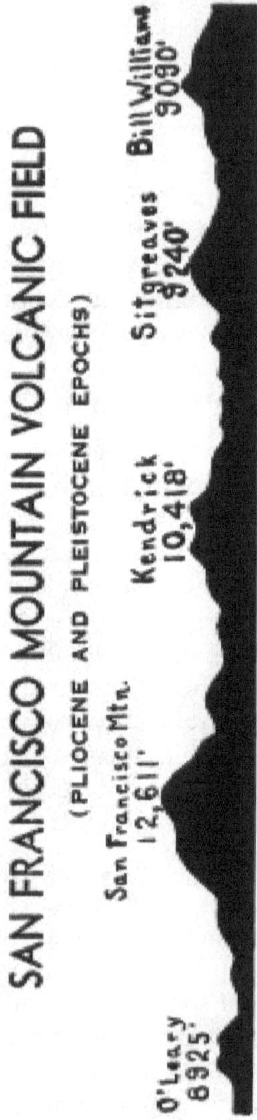

VIEW OF VOLCANOES FROM NORTH

Over a large part of the great plateau of northern Arizona are found sheets of hard lava and cone-shaped craters. The center of this volcanic activity is located in the San Francisco Peaks just north of the town of Flagstaff, but lavas and cones are found westward beyond Williams and to a considerable extent in every other direction. Looking south from Grand Canyon these peaks may be seen to rise high above the plateau and are a very beautiful sight. From Flagstaff and Williams not only the mountains but also great sheets of lava resting on the limestone surface are conspicuous.

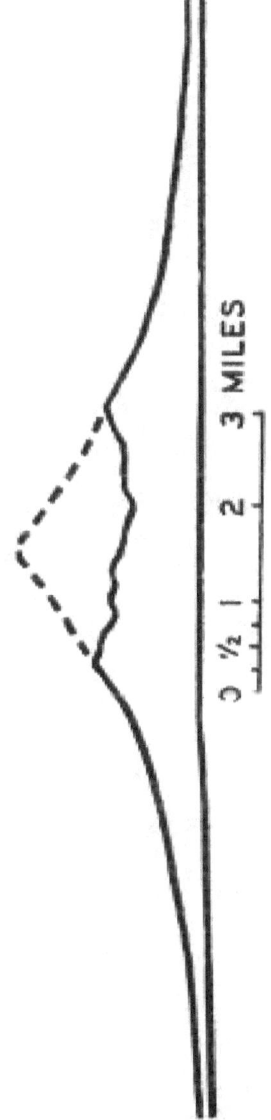

SAN FRANCISCO MOUNTAIN—PAST AND PRESENT

It was during the last great era in geological history, and for the most part after the Colorado River had already started to cut the Grand Canyon, that molten masses broke through and flowed out on the northern Arizona plateau. Three great periods of such volcanic activity are represented by the rocks of this region and they range in age from probably at least a million to relatively recent years.

The first general period of eruption in the San Francisco Volcanic Field was characterized by a predominance of lava flows which formed a black rock known as basalt. These flows had an average thickness of about 50 feet and covered an area of 3,000 square miles. Accompanying them was the formation of about a hundred small cinder cones.

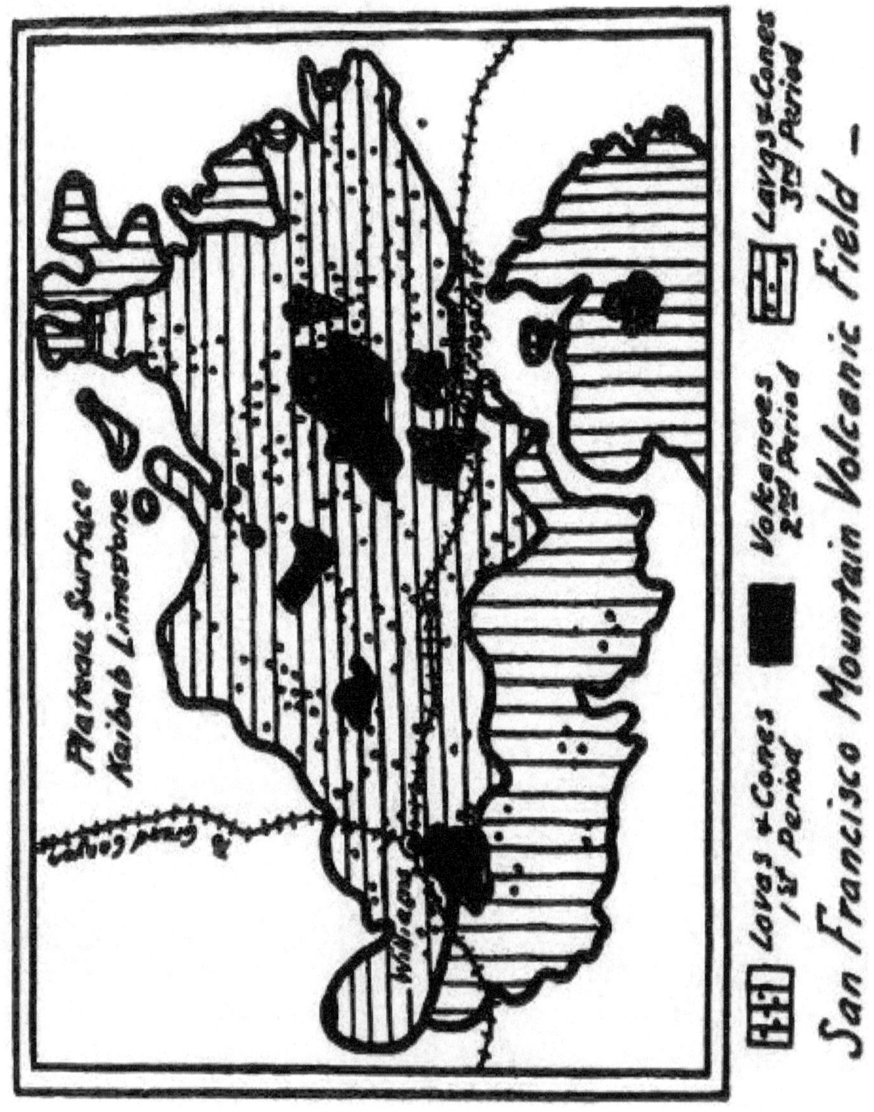

MAP OF SAN FRANCISCO MOUNTAIN VOLCANIC FIELD

It was during the second period of volcanism that six isolated cones of large size and a somewhat greater number of small cones were formed by the eruption of lavas widely ranging in composition. San Francisco Peak, the largest of these cones and a dominant feature of the region reaches an elevation of 12,611 feet above sea level, or about 5,000 feet above the plateau surface. It is composed of five different types, of lava—mostly red or light colored—which represent a corresponding number of distinct stages in eruption. Since the termination of its building-up, the crest of this cone has been eroded and worn away to the extent of 3,000 feet as estimated from restored cross-sections. Other large volcanic craters of this period are Bill Williams (9,090 feet), Kendrick (10,418 feet), O'Leary (8,925 feet) and Sitgreaves (9,240 feet).

Two hundred small cones and about twenty cubic miles of lava were produced in this same general region during a third and relatively recent period of volcanic activity. Much of this material overlies that of the two preceding periods. Probably the most interesting feature of these cones and flows is their age, at least one cone being so recent that ash from it buried numerous pithouses built by Pueblo Indians during the eleventh century, A. D.

SAN FRANCISCO MOUNTAIN

ELEPHANTS AND CAMELS (PLEISTOCENE EPOCH)

It was during the fifth and last great era in the earth's history that mammals developed and that man made his appearance on earth. In many places in the world the remains of animals that lived during various parts of this age have been preserved. In the famous asphalt pits of California literally hundreds of the bones of large mammals—tigers, mastodons, wolves and many others—have been brought to light. In the receding ice of northern Siberia, large mammoths—elephant-like animals representative of the last era, but unknown today—have come to the surface with even their skin and flesh preserved. But in the Grand Canyon region few fossils of the more recent times remain to tell the story of the life that then roamed over this surface. For long ages this region has been above the level of the sea, erosion has been continuous, so sediments have not accumulated and consequently few records of life have been made.

Recently near the western Navajo Indian agency at Tuba City, Arizona, however, the remains of several extinct animals were discovered. In a spring, hidden in a sandstone crevice, were found the tusks of a mammoth and some teeth which belonged to camels and bison. These were creatures native to this country not far back in history. They give but a very fragmentary insight into the more recent geologic history of the region, but they open up a field for interesting speculation to the imaginative person.

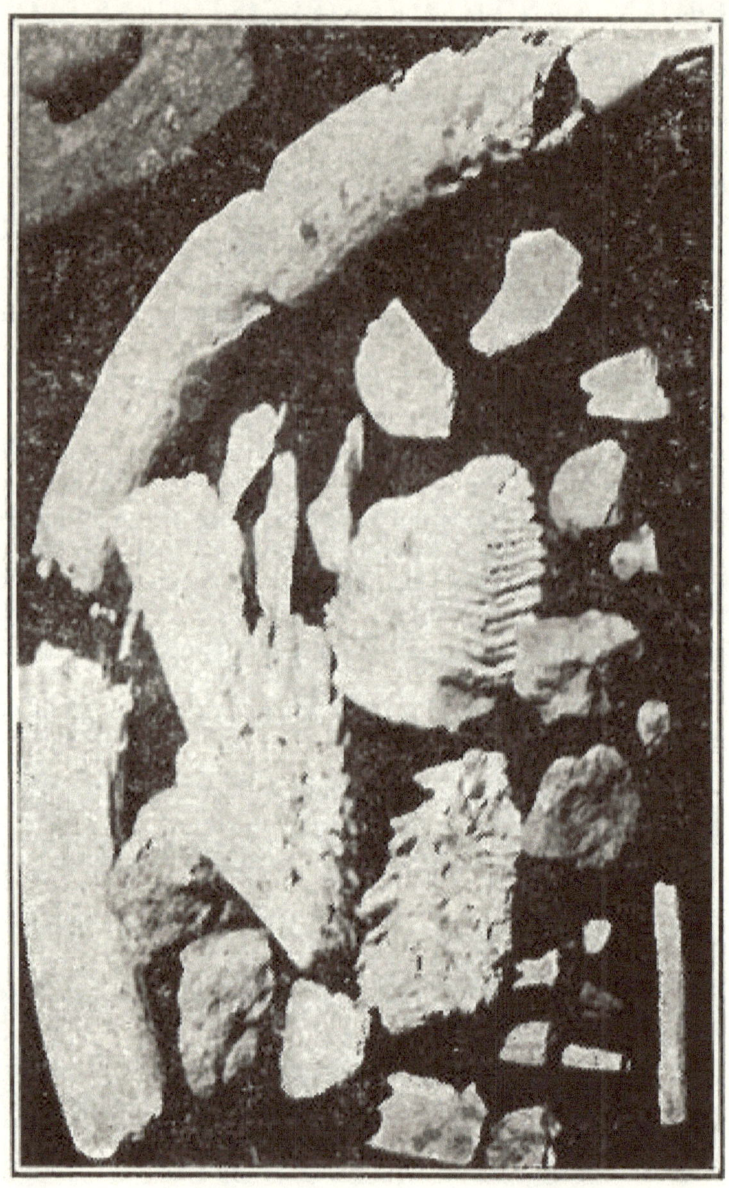

ELEPHANT AND CAMEL REMAINS

ADVENT OF MAN IN THE SOUTHWEST (PLEISTOCENE HISTORIC)

After reviewing the chapters of the earth's history and witnessing the procession and the slow but steady development of life through the ages, it is very natural that one should wonder when man came upon the scene. Compared with the hundreds of millions of years which have elapsed since the time of the first plants, or the millions of years following the first appearance of vertebrate animals, the age of man is as nothing. In the Old World there is evidence that humans existed before the last great Ice Ages, more than a million years ago, but in the Americas human occupation is measured in terms of thousands of years only.

Numerous recent discoveries in widely scattered parts of the Southwest indicate that man first occupied this region at a time when it was still inhabited by such animals as the ground sloth, the mammoth and the camel. Artifacts of stone and bone have been found associated with the remains of these animals. Early man's camp sites are located along the margins of former extensive water bodies that existed throughout this region at a time when the climate was far more humid than now. Little is known about the nature or habits of these men, but it is supposed that they were hunters with no knowledge of agriculture.

In the Grand Canyon region, the earliest human history with a clear, detailed record goes back only to about 300 A. D. From that time up to the present, however, the story of a flourishing and rapidly changing civilization is well recorded. Although no written documents have been left, abundant reliable information is available as a result of archeological excavations. Even the dates of many important events have been accurately determined through an ingenious method of calculating years on the basis of growth rings in the trees used for house construction.

**ANCIENT INDIAN PETROGLYPHS, HEAD OF BRIGHT ANGEL TRAIL,
GRAND CANYON**

Two distinct cultures are represented in the people who have inhabited the
Grand Canyon region for the past 1,600 years. The earlier and more primitive was
that of a long-headed type of man known as the Basketmaker. This culture was

replaced at about 700 A. D. by another, probably the result of new people entering the area, mixing with the older inhabitants and introducing new ideas. A broad-headed type of man who lived in pueblos and made pottery was the result. In the earliest stages he built only small one-roomed houses and made relatively crude pottery, but by 1,200 A. D. his architecture and crafts had developed to a very high stage as witnessed in the largest cliff-dwellings and pueblos of the region. Since then the culture has declined. The Hopi Indians of today who live near the Painted Desert Country to the east of Grand Canyon are considered to be modern representatives of this group.

In numerous localities throughout southern Utah burials of the early Farmer Basketmaker period and also pithouses of the later Potter Basketmaker period have been found. One of the latter has also been discovered near Clear Creek in Grand Canyon. The remains of cliff-dwellings and surface houses built by the later Pueblo Indians are common everywhere throughout the region and show all stages of development. Those at and in the Grand Canyon are typical of the intermediate periods and, judging from pottery fragments in them, were made by the ancestors of the modern Hopi.

GEOLOGICAL BIBLIOGRAPHY OF GRAND CANYON REGION

INCLUDING ZION, BRYCE, PAINTED DESERT, AND PETRIFIED FOREST

Allen, V. T., Triassic Bentonite of the Painted Desert: Am. Jour. Sci., vol. xix, April, 1930.

Baker, A. A. and others, Notes on the Stratigraphy of the Moab Region, Utah; Bull. Am. Assoc. Petrol. Geol., vol. 11, 1927.

— — and Reeside, J. B., Correlation of the Permian of southern Utah, northern Arizona, northwestern New Mexico, and southwestern Colorado: Bull. Am. Assoc. Petrol. Geol., vol. 13, no. 11, Nov., 1929.

— —, Dane, C. H., and Reeside, J. B. Jr., Correlation of the Jurassic Formations of Parts of Utah, Arizona, New Mexico and Colorado: U. S. Geol. Survey Prof. Paper 183, 1936.

— —, Geology of the Monument Valley—Navajo Mountain Region, San Juan County, Utah: U. S. Geol. Survey Bull. 865, 1936.

Brady, L. F., Preliminary Note on the Occurrence of a Primitive Theropod in the Navajo: Amer. Jour. Sci., vol. 30, 1935.

Branson, E. B., and Mehl, M. G., Triassic Amphibians from the Rocky Mountain Region: Univ. Mo. Studies, vol. 4, no. 2, 1929.

Butler, B. S., The Ore Deposits of Utah: U. S. Geol. Survey Prof. Paper 111, pp. 619-620, 1920.

Bryan, Kirk, Discussion of rock-fill dam, Lees Ferry, Arizona: Am. Soc. Civ. Eng., Proc., vol. 48, pp. 1615-1627.

— —, Wind Erosion near Lees Ferry, Arizona: Am. Jour. Sci., vol. 6, p. 291, 1923.

Camp, Charles L., A Study of the Phytosaurs: Memoirs, Univ. Calif., vol. 10, Univ. Calif. Press, 1930.

— — and VanderHoof, V. L., Small Bipedal Dinosaur from the Jurassic of Northern Arizona: Proc. Geol. Soc. Amer., abstract, pp. 384-5, 1934.

Campbell, Ian, and Maxson, J. H., Some Observations on the Archean Metamorphics of the Grand Canyon: Proc. Nat. Acad. Sci., vol. 19, no. 9, pp. 806-809,

1933.

Campbell, M. R., and Gregory, H. E., The Black Mesa coal field, Arizona: U. S. Geol. Survey Bull. 431, pt. 2, 1909.

Carpenter, Frank M., A Fossil Insect from the Lower Permian of the Grand Canyon: U. S. National Museum Proc. No. 2695, 1927.

Colton, Harold S., Sunset Crater—The Effect of a Volcanic Eruption on an Ancient Pueblo People: Geogr. Review, vol. 22, no. 4, 1932.

— — Basaltic Cinder Cones and Lava Flows of the San Francisco Mountain Volcanic Field: Mus. Northern Arizona, Bull. 10, 1937.

Cross and Howe, Redbeds of southwestern Colorado and their correlation: Geol. Soc. Am. Bull., vol. 16, pp. 486-487, 1905.

Dake, C. L., The pre-Moencopi unconformity of the Colorado Plateau: Jour. Geology, vol. 28, pp. 61-74, 1920.

Darton, N. H., Reconnaissance of parts of northwestern New Mexico and northern Arizona: U. S. Geol. Survey, Bull. 435, 84 pp., 17 pls., 1910.

— — Guidebook of the western United States: Part C, the Santa Fe Route with a side trip to the Grand Canyon of the Colorado: U. S. Geol. Survey Bull. 615, pp. 123-131, 1915.

— — A Reconnaissance of parts of northwestern New Mexico and northern Arizona: U. S. Geol. Surv. Prof. Paper 131, 1922.

— — Resume of Arizona geology: Arizona Bu. of Mines, Bull. 119, 1925.

Daugherty, Lyman H., New Fossil Plants from the Petrified Forest: Proc. Geol. Soc. Amer., abstract, p. 389, 1934.

Davis, W. M., Notes on the Colorado Canyon district: Am. Jour. Sci., 4th ser., vol. 10, pp. 251-259, 1900.

— — An excursion to the Grand Canyon of the Colorado: Harvard Coll. Mus. Comp. Zool., vol. 38, pp. 107-201, 1901.

— — The lessons of the Colorado Canyon: Bull. Am. Geogr. Soc., vol. 41, 1909.

Diller, J. S., Asbestos in 1917: U. S. Geol. Survey Mineral Resources of U. S. 1917, Pt. 2, pp. 198-199, 1918.

Dutton, E. C., The physical history of the Grand Canyon District: U. S. Geol. Survey Second Ann. Rept., pp. 47-166, pls. X-XXV, and map, 1882.

— — Tertiary history of the Grand Canyon District: U. S. Geol. Survey Mon. 2, 264 pp., folio atlas, 1882.

Frech, F., Section in Congress Canyon opposite Point Sublime: Compt. rend. 5th Sess. Cong. geol. internat., pp. 476-81, 1893.

Gilbert, G. K., Report on the geology of portions of Nevada, Utah, California, and Arizona, examined in the years 1871, 1872, and 1873, Report U. S. Geog. Surveys W. 100th Mer. vol. 3, pp. 17-187, 503-567, 1875.

Gilmore, Charles W., Fossil Footprints from the Grand Canyon: Smithsonian Misc. Collections 77 No. 9, 80 No. 3, 80 No. 8, 1926-7-8.

Gregory, H. E., Geology of the Navajo Country: U. S. Geol. Survey Prof. Paper 93, 161 pp., map, 1917.

— — The Shinarump conglomerate: Am. Jour. Sci., vol. 35, pp. 424-438, 1913.

— — Reconnaissance of a portion of the Little Colorado Valley: Am. Jour. Sci., 4th ser., vol. 38, pp. 491-501.

— — Igneous origin of the glacial deposits of the Navajo Reservation: Am. Jour. Sci., 4th ser., vol. 40, pp. 97-115.

— — The Navajo Country: U. S. Geol. Survey Water-Supply Paper 380, 219 pp., map, 1916.

— — and Moore, R. C., The Kaiparowits Region: U. S. Geol. Surv. Prof. Paper 164, 161 pp. 31 pls., 1931.

— —, Colorado Plateau Region, xvi International Geological Congress, Guidebook 18, Excursions C-1, C-2, 1933.

Hager, Dorsey, Stratigraphy—northeast Arizona—southeast Utah: Mining and Oil Bull., vol. 10, pp. 167, 423, 1924.

Hesse, Curtis J., Semionotus cf., gigas, from the Triassic of Zion Park, Utah: Amer. Jour. Sci., vol. 29, 1935.

Hinds, Norman E. A., Ep-Archean and Ep-Algonkian Intervals in Western North America: Carnegie Inst. Washington, Publ. No. 463, pp. 1-52, 1935.

— — Uncompahgran and Beltian Deposits in Western North America: Carnegie Inst. Washington, Publ. No. 463, pp. 53-136, 1936.

Huntington, Ellsworth and Goldthwait, J. W., The Hurricane Fault in the Toquerville district, Utah: Harvard Coll. Mus. Comp. Zool. Bull., vol. 42, 1904.

Iddings, J. P., Pre-Cambrian igneous rocks of the Unkar terrane, Grand Canyon of the Colorado, Ariz., by C. D. Walcott, with notes on the petrographic character of the lavas by Iddings U. S. Geol. Survey Fourteenth Ann. Report, Part 2, pp. 520-24, 1895.

Johnson, D. W., A geological excursion in the Grand Canyon district: Proc. Boston Soc. Nat. Hist., vol. 34, pp. 135-161, pls. 17-22, 1909.

Knowlton, F. H., The Fossil Forests of Arizona: Amer. For., vol. 9, 1913.

— — A Catalogue of the Mesozoic and Cenozoic plants of North America: U. S. Geol. Survey Bull. 696, 1919.

Lee, W. T., Geologic reconnaissance of a part of western Arizona: U. S. Geol. Survey Bull. 352, 96 pp., 11 pls. 1908.

— Stories in Stone. C. Van Nostrand Co., 1926.

— — The Canyons and Painted Cliffs of Zion National Park and the Story of their Origin, National Park Service.

Longwell, C. R., Geology of the Muddy Mountains, Nev., with a section to the Grand Wash Cliffs, in western Arizona: Am. Jour. Sci., 4th ser., vol. 50, pp. 52-54, 1921.

— — and others, Rock formations in the Colorado Plateau of southeastern Utah and northern Arizona: U. S. Geol. Survey Prof. Paper 132, pp. 1-23, 1923.

— —, The pre-Triassic unconformity in southern Nevada: Am. Jour. Sci., 5th ser., vol. 10, pp. 93-106, 1925.

— — Structural studies in southern Nevada and western Arizona: Geol. Soc. Am. Bull., vol. 37, pp. 551-584, pls. 17-20, 1926.

— —, Geology of the Muddy Mountains, Nevada, with a section through the Virgin Range to the Grand Wash Cliffs, Arizona: U. S. Geol. Survey Bull. 798, 1928.

— —, Geology of the Boulder Reservoir Floor: Bull. Geol. Soc. Amer., vol. 47, pp. 1393-1476, 1936.

Lucas, F. A., Vertebrates from the Trias of Arizona: Science, new ser., vol. 14, p. 376, 1901.

— — A New Batrachian and a new reptile from the Trias of Arizona: U. S. Nat. Mus. Proc., vol. 27, pp. 193, 195, 1904.

Lull, R. S., Fossil Footprints from the Grand Canyon of the Colorado: Amer. Jour. Sci., vol. 45, 1918.

Marcou, Jules, Resume and field notes: U. S. Pacific Railroad Expl. vol. 3, pt. 4. Geological Report, 1856.

Matthes, F. E., Bright Angel Quadrangle. U. S. Geol. Survey topo. map text.

Marvine, A. R., Report on the geology of the route from St. George Utah, to Gila River, Arizona, examined in 1871: U. S. Geog. Survey W. of 100th Mer., vol. 3, 1875, pp. 189-225, maps.

Maxson, J. H., and Campbell, Ian, Archean Ripple Mark in the Grand Canyon: Amer. Jour. Sci., vol. 28, 1934.

McKee, Edwin D., Climates of the Age of Mammals in the Grand Canyon Region: Museum Notes, Museum of Northern Arizona, Flagstaff, 1932.

— —, Arizona Through the Ages: Scientific Monthly, 1932.

— — The Coconino Sandstone—Its History and Origin: Carnegie Institution Publ. 440, vii, 1934.

— — A Study of the Light-colored, Cross-bedded Sandstones of Canyon de Chelly, Arizona: Am. Jour. Sci., 5th Ser., vol. 28, pp. 219-233, 1934.

— —, Occurrence of Triassic Sediments on the Rim of Grand Canyon: Jour. Wash. Acad. Sci., vol. 25, no. 4, 1935.

— —, A Conularia from the Permian of Arizona: Jour. Paleontology, vol. 9, no. 5, 1935.

— —, Triassic Pebbles in Northern Arizona Containing Invertebrate Fossils:

Amer. Jour. Sci., vol. 33, 1937.

— —, The Environment and History of the Toroweap and Kaibab formations of Northern Arizona and Southern Utah: Carnegie Inst. Washington, Publ. 492, 1938.

Merriam, John C., The Living Past, Charles Scribner's Sons, 1930.

Miller, W. J., Zion Canyon National Park, Utah: Journal of Geography, May, 1923.

Moore, R. C., On the Stratigraphy of Northeastern Arizona: Am. Assoc. Petrol. Geol. Bull., vol. 6, no. 1, pp. 47-49, 1922.

Newberry, J. S., Report upon the Colorado River of the West, explored in 1857-58 by Lieut. J. C. Ives: Govt. Printing Office, pt. 3, Geological Report, 1861.

Noble, L. F., The geology of the Shinumo area: Am. Jour. Sci., 4th ser., vol. 29, pp. 369-386, 497-528, 1910.

— —, The Shinumo Quadrangle, Grand Canyon district, Arizona: U. S. Geol. Survey Bull. 549, 100 pp., 18 pls., 1914.

— — A Section of the Paleozoic formations of the Grand Canyon on the Bass Trail: U. S. Geol. Survey Prof. Paper 131, pp. 23-73, 1922.

— — and Hunter, J. F., A reconnaissance of the Archean complex of the Granite Gorge, Grand Canyon, Arizona: U. S. Geol. Survey Prof. Paper 98, pp. 95-113, 1916.

— — A Section of Kaibab Limestone in Kaibab Gulch, Utah: U. S. Geol. Survey, Prof. Paper 150, 1928.

Powell, J. W., Exploration of the Colorado River of the West and its tributaries explored in 1869-1872: Smithsonian Inst., 291 pp., 1873.

Ransome, F. L., Pre-Cambrian in Grand Canyon: Science, vol. 27, pp. 667-668, 1908.

— — Some Paleozoic sections in Arizona and their correlations: U. S. Geol. Survey Prof. Paper 98, pp. 133-166, 1916.

Reagan, Albert B., Some Geological Notes on the Upper Cretaceous of Black Mesa, Arizona, Transactions of the Kansas Academy of Science, vol. 35, pp. 232-252, 1932.

— — The Tertiary—Pleistocene of the Navajo Country in Arizona, with a description of some of its included fossils: Transactions of the Kansas Academy of Science, vol. 35, pp. 253-259, 1932.

Reeside, J. B., and Bassler, Harvey, Stratigraphic sections in southwestern Utah and northwestern Arizona: U. S. Geol. Sur. Prof. Paper, 129-D, 1922.

Robinson, H. H., The San Franciscan volcanic field, Arizona: U. S. Geol. Survey Prof. Paper 76, 213 pp., 14 pls., 1913.

Schuchert, Charles, On the Carboniferous of the Grand Canyon—The Cambrian of the Grand Canyon: Am. Jour. Sci., 4th ser., vol. 45, pp. 347-369, 1918.

Shimer, H. W., Permo-Triassic of northwestern Arizona: Geol. Soc. Am. Bull., vol. 30, 1919.

Stoyanow, A. A., Notes on recent stratigraphic work in Arizona: Am. Jour. Sci., vol. 12, pp. 311-324, 1926.

— —, Correlation of Arizona Paleozoic Formations: Bull. Geol. Soc. Amer., vol. 47, pp. 459-540, 1936.

Vander Hoof, V. L., The Chinle Formation: Museum Notes, Mus. Northern Arizona, vol. 6, no. 7, 1934.

Walcott, C. D., The Permian and other Paleozoic groups of the Kanab Valley, Arizona: Am. Jour. Sci., 3rd ser., vol. 20, pp. 221-225, 1880.

— — Pre-Carboniferous strata in the Grand Canyon of the Colorado, Ariz.: Am. Jour. Sci., 3rd ser., vol. 26, pp. 437, 442, 484, 1883; U. S. Geol. Survey Fourth Ann. Rept., p. 47, 1884.

— — Study of a line of displacement in the Grand Canyon in northeast Arizona: Bull. Geol. Soc. America, vol. 1, pp. 49-64, 1890.

— — Pre-Cambrian igneous rocks of the Unkar terrane, Grand Canyon of the Colorado, Ariz., with notes on the petrographic character of the Lavas, by J. P. Iddings: U. S. Geol. Survey Fourteenth Ann. Rept. Pt. 2, pp. 497-524, 1894.

— — Algonkian rocks of the Grand Canyon of the Colorado: Jour. Geology, vol. 3, pp. 312-330, pls. 6, 1895.

— — Pre-Cambrian fossiliferous formations: Bull. Geol. Soc. America, vol. 10, pp. 199-244, 1899.

— — Cambrian geology and paleontology: Smithsonian Misc. Coll., vol. 64, no. 5, pp. 373, 374, 1916.

— —, Geology of the Little Colorado Valley: Am. Jour. Sci., 4th ser., vol. 12, pp. 401-413, 1901.

Ward, L. F., Report on the Petrified Forest of Arizona: Twentieth Ann. Rept., U. S. Geol. Survey, Pt. II, pp. 324-332, 1900.

— — The Petrified Forest of Arizona: Smith Rept. for 1899, Wash., pp. 289-307, 1901.

White, David, Study of the fossil floras in the Grand Canyon: Carnegie Inst. Year-Book 26, pp. 366-369, 1927.

— — Flora of the Hermit Shale, Grand Canyon, Ariz., Publication No. 405 Carnegie Institution, 1929.

Williams, Howell, Pliocene Volcanoes of the Navajo-Hopi Country: Bull. Geol. Soc. Amer., vol. 47, pp. 111-172, 1936.

Lector House believes that a society develops through a two-fold approach of continuous learning and adaptation, which is derived from the study of classic literary works spread across the historic timeline of literature records. Therefore, we aim at reviving, repairing and redeveloping all those inaccessible or damaged but historically as well as culturally important literature across subjects so that the future generations may have an opportunity to study and learn from past works to embark upon a journey of creating a better future.

This book is a result of an effort made by Lector House towards making a contribution to the preservation and repair of original ancient works which might hold historical significance to the approach of continuous learning across subjects.

HAPPY READING & LEARNING!

LECTOR HOUSE LLP
E-MAIL: lectorpublishing@gmail.com